CODING UNPLUGGED

CODING WITH NUMBER PLAY

GETTING KID-CODERS OFF THE SCREEN AND ON THEIR FEET!

BY KAITLYN SIU

ILLUSTRATED BY DAVE SMITH

WARNING

WARNING: You should have the help of an adult when putting together and performing any activity. If you are allergic to any of the materials, you should not use it.

Please visit our website, www.garethstevens.com. For a free color catalog of all our high-quality books, call toll free 1-800-542-2595 or fax 1-877-542-2596.

Cataloging-in-Publication Data
Names: Siu, Kaitlyn, author. | Smith, Dave, illustrator.
Title: Coding with number play / Kaitlyn Siu , illustrated by Dave Smith.
Description: Buffalo, NY : Gareth Stevens Publishing, 2026. |
Series: Coding unplugged | Includes glossary and index.
Identifiers: ISBN 9781482473780 (pbk.) | ISBN 9781482473797 (library bound) |
ISBN 9781482473803 (ebook)
Subjects: LCSH: Computer programming--Juvenile literature. |
Coding theory--Juvenile literature.
Classification: LCC QA76.6115 S58 2026 | DDC 005.13--dc23

Published in 2026 by
Gareth Stevens Publishing
2544 Clinton St.
Buffalo, NY 14224

First published in Great Britain in 2023 by Wayland

Commissioning Editor: Grace Glendinning
Project Manager: Em Stafford
Designer: Emma DeBanks
Illustrations: Dave Smith

Printed in the United States of America

CPSIA compliance information: Batch #CSGS26: For further information contact Gareth Stevens at 1-800-542-2595.

Find us on

CONTENTS

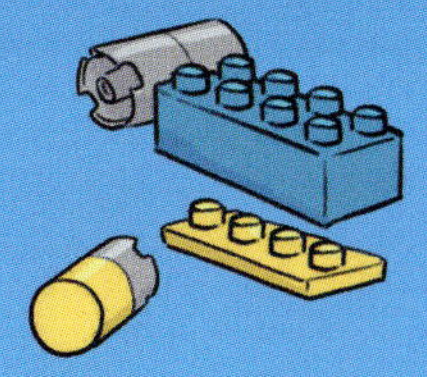

SCREEN-FREE CODING
WITH SIMPLE NUMBER PLAY

Let's go on a **CODING ADVENTURE** with **NUMBERS!** We're going to learn how to talk like computers with fun math-style activities you can do almost anywhere.

The activities in this book are all **UNPLUGGED**, which means you don't need a computer or a screen to learn how to code. Most of them involve getting together with friends and using teamwork, taking it all outside if you like to get lots of fresh air!

You'll be a robot one minute and constructing a tower the next. You won't believe where you can find coding at work–or how much fun number play can be!

WHAT IS **CODING?**

Coding is the process of giving computers **INSTRUCTIONS** in a language they understand. Computers are not naturally smart. If it's raining outside, a computer doesn't automatically know it needs an umbrella.

It needs to be given very specific instructions to perform even basic tasks.

By the end of this book, you're going to be talking in **"COMPUTER."** You'll know how to give computers instructions that they will understand, using some of the math facts you already know.

CAN YOU SEE?

Did you know that coding with numbers is everywhere? Coding is the backbone of so many things we use on a daily basis. We wouldn't be able to understand a crosswalk signal, use an elevator, or follow a GPS without coding!

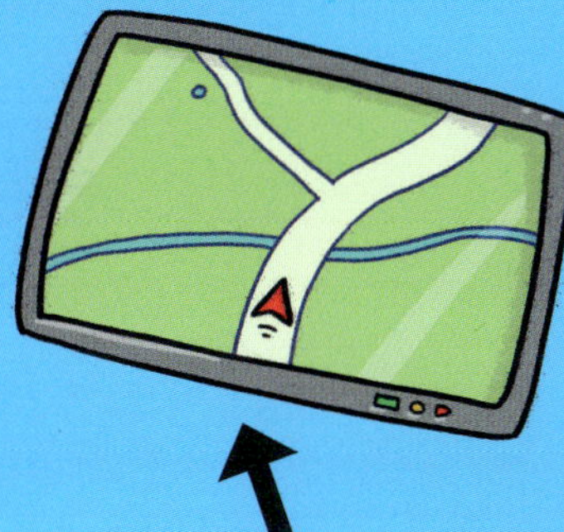

KIDS CAN CODE

You don't need to be a computer programmer to learn the basic concepts of coding. In fact, there are **6 SIMPLE CODING TOOLS** that form the foundation of code, which you can learn at any age–and with **NO SCREEN** at all!

CODING CONCEPTS

You may know some of these already, but you can turn the page to remind yourself, or use the next few pages as quick references when you start the **ACTIVITIES** later in the book.

KEY CODING CONCEPT #1:
THE ALGORITHM

An **ALGORITHM** is an **INSTRUCTION** given to help complete a certain task.

We can think of an algorithm like a **RECIPE**. You need to follow a set of **INSTRUCTIONS** to bake the perfect cake. It's important to read the instructions carefully. If you accidentally set the oven to the wrong temperature your cake won't turn out right!

We use an algorithm when we are adding big numbers called the **LONG ADDITION METHOD**. This method first breaks the numbers into **PAIRS**, and then adds up the pairs, one at a time. By following this algorithm we can add together any two numbers!

KEY CODING CONCEPT #2: SEQUENCE

SEQUENCE refers to your algorithm's **ORDER** of steps.

When you give **INSTRUCTIONS**, it's important to give them in the **CORRECT ORDER**. It wouldn't make sense to put your shoes on before your socks or your jeans before your underwear.

If you are following a **MAP** you'll need to walk the **DIRECTIONS** in the **CORRECT ORDER** or you'll end up in the wrong spot. You'll need to use your math skills to count out the correct number of steps in each direction.

KEY CODING CONCEPT #3: LOOPS

A loop is a **SET** of **INSTRUCTIONS** that repeat and repeat until a specific condition is met.

When you open up a tablet, you might be asked for a **PASSWORD**.

Computers are programmed to ask you for your password again and again until the correct password is typed in. This helps to keep the information on your tablet safe!

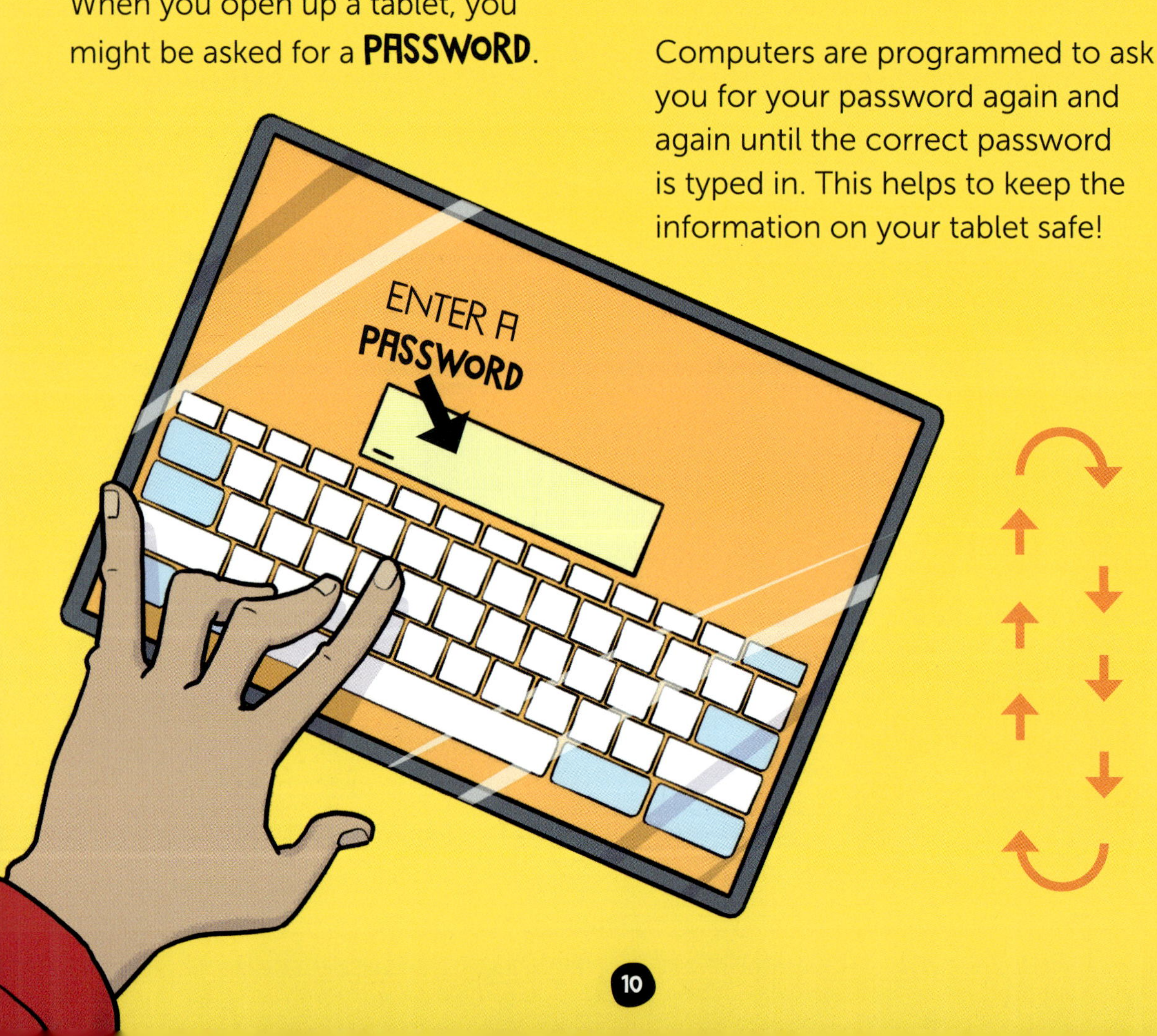

KEY CODING CONCEPT #4:
VARIABLES

A variable is a way of **HOLDING INFORMATION**. It's like a box that keeps information inside it.

Variables can be **REPRESENTED** with **LETTERS, WORDS,** or **NUMBERS**. When playing basketball we can think of the score as a variable. The scoreboard holds a number and that number can change depending on how many baskets the players score.

KEY CODING CONCEPT #5: BRANCHING

Branching refers to making a **DECISION** based on what is **HAPPENING** or **HAS HAPPENED**.

Computers make decisions **BASED** on these **CONDITIONS** all the time, just like we do with the weather, for example.

If the weather is **40°F (5°C)**, we should put on **A JACKET**.

If the weather is **85°F (30°C)**, we should put on **SHORTS** and a **T-SHIRT**.

KEY CODING CONCEPT #6: DECOMPOSITION

Decomposition refers to breaking something up into **SMALLER PARTS**.

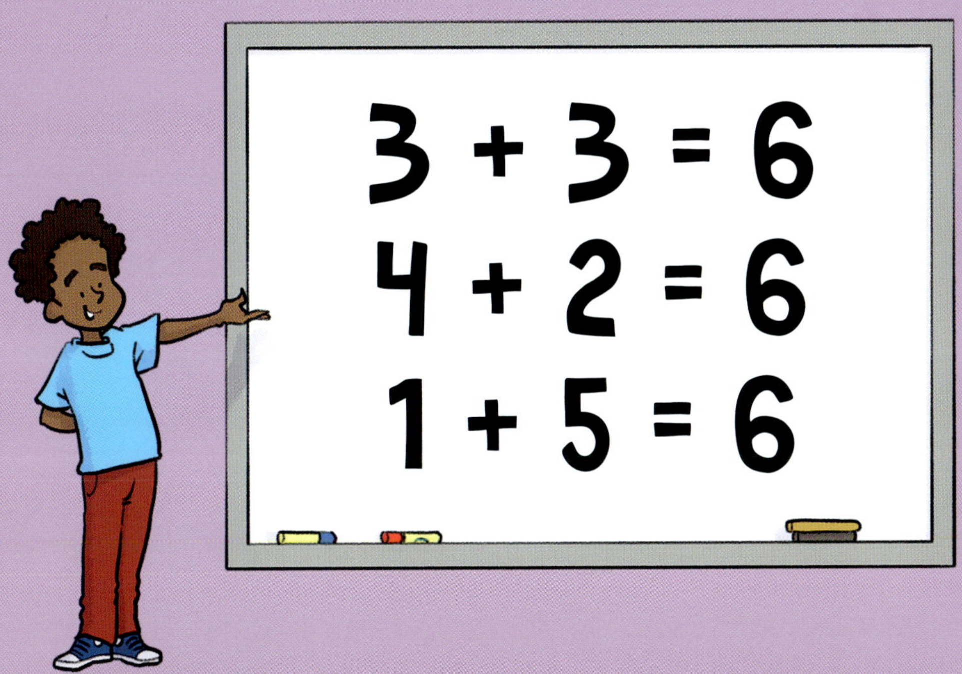

15

We can use decomposition to help us come up with simple math problems. We can make the number 6 by adding 3+3, 4+2, and 5+1. How many ways can you think of to get to the number 15 by adding two numbers together?

(ANSWER ON PAGE 48)

ALGORITHMS UNPLUGGED:
ROBOT HOPSCOTCH

Designing a **HOPSCOTCH MAZE** and pretending to be **ROBOTS** following code is a great way to practice **WRITING** and **SEQUENCING** an algorithm.

So, let's **GET OUTSIDE** and hop around!

In this activity, we will program a "robot" to get from **START** to **FINISH** ... with a little bit of silliness along the way! We'll also practice looking out for **BUGS** in our code. *Bug-free code earns more points!*

MATERIALS YOU WILL NEED:

- At least 5 colors of chalk
- A paved surface outside in a safe place
- One die
- At least two amazing coder brains!

SETTING UP:

1. Draw a square grid on your paved surface using chalk (such as 10 x 10 or 15 x 15).

2. Place an **S** for **START** at one corner and an **F** for **FINISH** at the farthest corner, opposite.

3. Mark the sides of your grid: **LEFT**, **RIGHT**, **TOP**, and **BOTTOM**, like this:

TOP

LEFT

RIGHT

BOTTOM

4. Using all the colored chalk, color in 20 random grid spaces.

   ✱ These are your activity squares! If you land on one, you must perform an action in a loop before you can move on.

5. Brainstorm activities for each colored square and write them out as a key. For example:

   Pink square = **JUMPING JACKS**
   Green square = **SILLY DANCE MOVES**
   Orange square = **BEHIND-THE-BACK CLAPS**

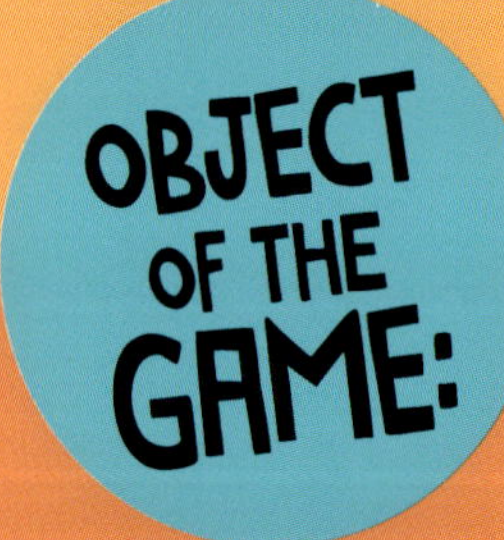

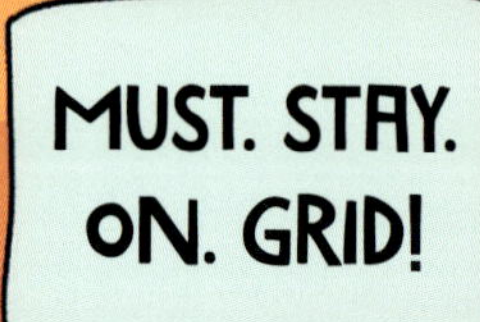

✱ Teams (or players) **TAKE TURNS** to be "**CODERS**" and "**ROBOTS**."

✱ Each will get **THREE TURNS** as coder to score points, and three turns as robot to follow their opponents' algorithm. After all six algorithms are completed, the team with the most points **WINS**!

✱ A **SUCCESSFUL** algorithm keeps the robot in the grid at all times, and reaches the **FINISH** at the end of the algorithm.

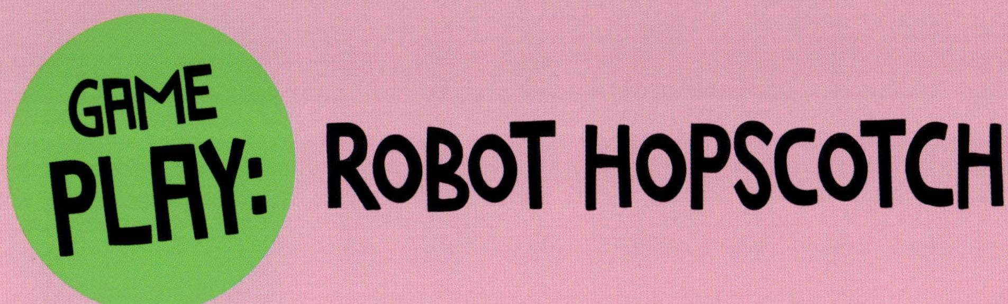

1. Roll to see who codes first.

2. Each algorithm round works like this:

   * Roll the die to decide how many squares to hop. This can be broken up if needed. For example, if you roll a 6, you can decide to do:
   three squares up and three squares left, or four up/two right, etc.

   * Write out each algorithm step using arrows written in chalk, like this, being sure to keep track of the roll for each step:

All algorithms must follow these rules:

* Stop on at least two activity squares along the way.
* Roll until you think you've got an algorithm that finishes on the FINISH square.
* Write it out fully in advance, then "run the code" all at once when you think it's ready. No testing it out on the grid!

ONLY USE YOUR EYES AND CLEVER PLANNING SKILLS!

GAME PLAY: RUN THAT CODE

3. Once the coders have completed their algorithm, one person from **TEAM ROBOT** steps onto the **START** space.

4. The **CODING TEAM** can shout out their algorithm to direct the robot to hop across the grid.

5. When a player lands on an **ACTIVITY** square, roll the die to see how many times the robot must loop the action before moving on to the next step in the algorithm.

* For example, if a player rolls 5 on a **SILLY DANCE MOVE** space, then the player does a silly dance move five times.

* A successful algorithm on the first try earns **10 POINTS**.

* Debugged algorithms, successful on the second try, earn **5 POINTS**.

* **NO POINTS** for two failed algorithms!

GAME PLAY: DEBUG!

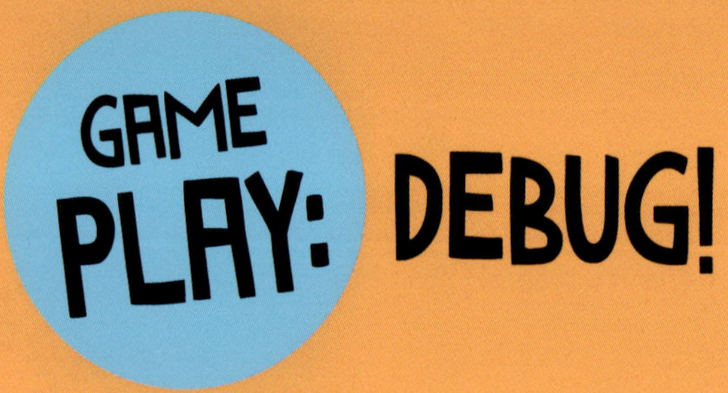

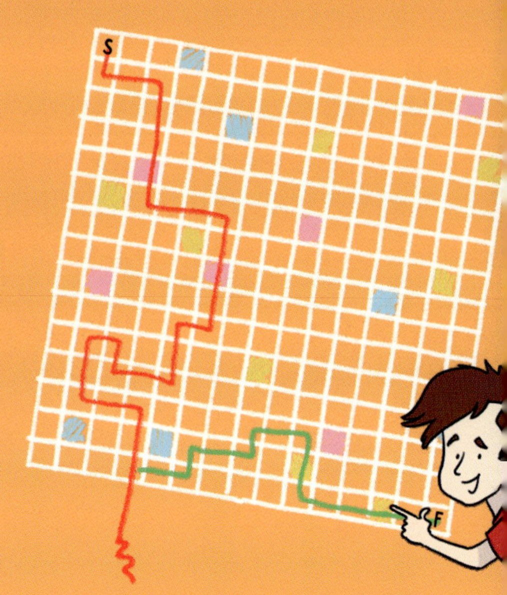

If there is a **MISTAKE** in the algorithm–if the robot "falls off" the grid or doesn't make it to the finish–the robot heads back to the **START** space and waits for the coders to **DEBUG** their algorithm.

* The coders must re-plan their steps using the **same** die rolls from this round.
* If they need more rolls at the end to get the robot all the way to the finish, they may add rolls as needed.
* So, in our example on page 17, they must still use the rolls **5, 2, 6, 5, 4** before they can roll more.

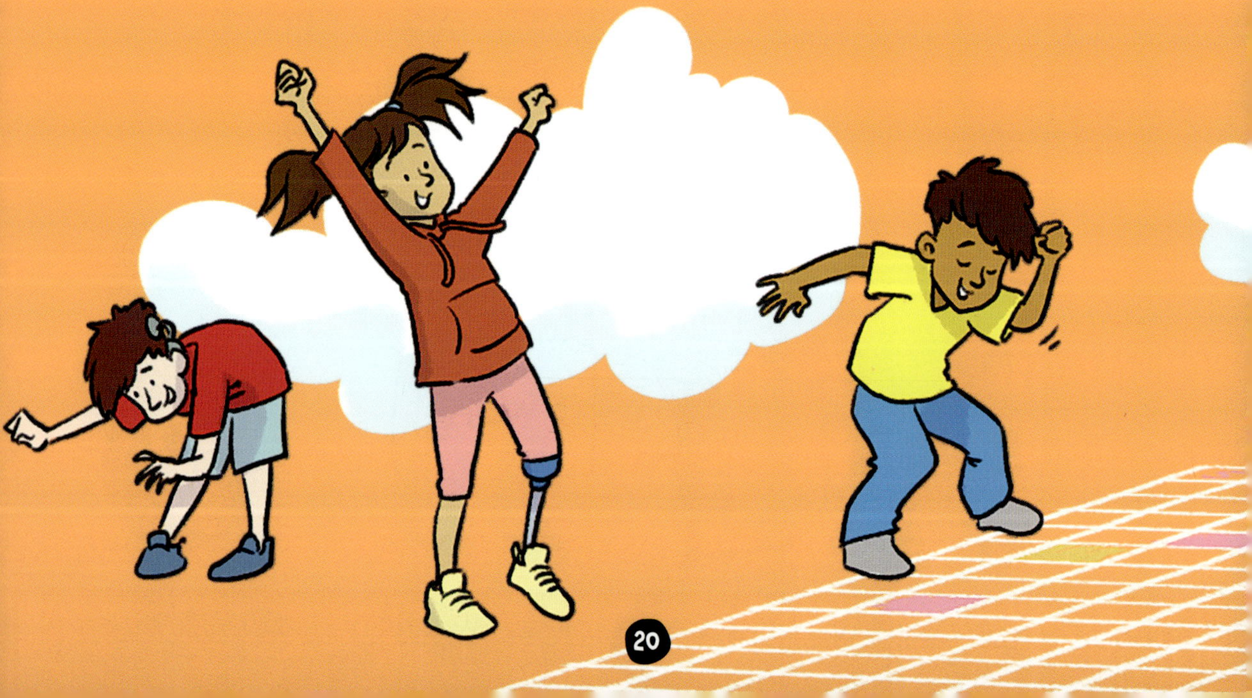

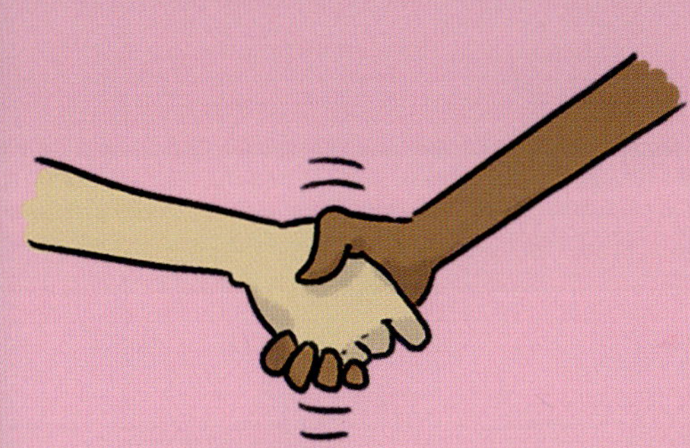

TiE BREAKER*

*YOU'LL NEED TO FIND A SECOND DIE TO ROLL IF IT COMES TO A TIE-BREAKER!

SPEED ROUND, where both teams plan an algorithm at the **SAME TIME** and "run" it using a member of their own team as soon as they are ready. The **FIRST TO THE FINISH** successfully wins!

TAKE TURNS. HAVE FUN. GET CODING!

SPOT THE CODE
Which coding concepts do you see at work here? Can you believe that math and coding are in use even when we exercise?!
(ANSWER ON PAGE 48)
TWENTY MORE REPS, THEN YOU'RE DONE!

REMEMBER THE ROUTINE, EVERYONE?
IF YOU ARE ABLE, HOLD FOR 60 SECONDS ON ELBOWS AND TOES. IF NOT, HANDS AND KNEES ARE JUST FINE!

LOOPS UNPLUGGED:
CODE A TIMED OBSTACLE COURSE

Coding an obstacle course is a great way to learn about **LOOPS** and **BRANCHES**. It's also a great way to have fun with your friends!

First, you'll practice writing an obstacle course algorithm, and then you'll add in some numbers-based loops and branches to make it trickier.

MATERIALS YOU WILL NEED:

- Dice
- A stopwatch or timer
- Pillows
- Plastic cups
- A broomstick
- Sofa cushions
- A flat, narrow board
- Hula hoops
- An adult to supervise

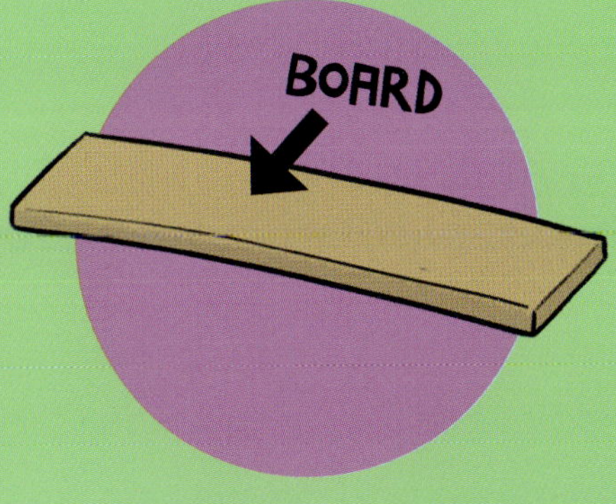

DESIGN YOUR **OBSTACLE COURSE** ALGORITHM

CHOOSE THREE TO FIVE OBSTACLES FROM THE SUGGESTIONS:

STATION ONE:

* **LIMBO:** Create a limbo station by holding up a broomstick. The goal is to get under the broomstick by arching backwards. Don't touch the broomstick on your way under!

STATION TWO:

* **HULA HOOPS:** Line up hula hoops side by side for a jumping challenge. The goal is to jump from one hoop to the next while keeping your feet inside the hoops. If you don't have hula hoops, you can draw circles with chalk.

STATION THREE:

* **TUNNEL:** If you don't have a play tunnel, you can use cushions or chairs to create a tunnel to crawl through. The goal is to get through the tunnel without it collapsing.

STATION FOUR:

* **ZIGZAG:** You can use plastic cups to create a zigzag path. The goal is to swerve from one object to the next as fast as you can as you move forwards.

STATION FIVE:

* **BALANCE BEAM:** If you don't have a flat piece of wood, you can use a curb outside or a line of books to create a low balance beam. The goal is to walk from one side to the other without falling off.

* Choose the order of your stations and label each with a number.
* Set up the materials needed for each station.
* Give each player one die–this will be used to program your loops and branches.

TIMED OBSTACLE COURSE

Now it's time to use our **CODING** and **MATH BRAINS** in our amazing obstacle course.

The player with the next birthday goes first.

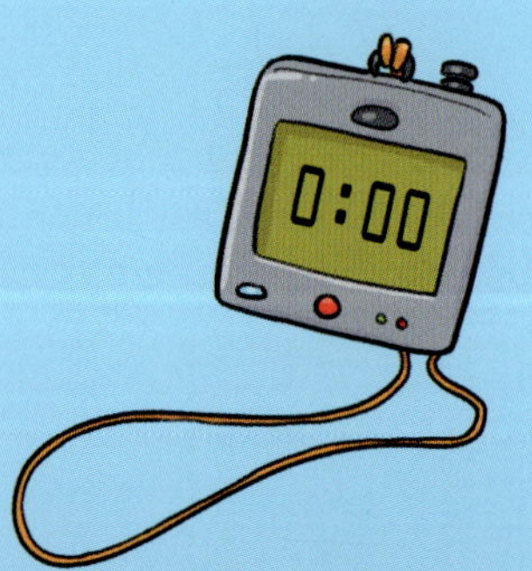

Start at station one. Have someone use a **STOPWATCH** to time each person's turn through the course.

Player one rolls their die. The **NUMBER** they roll represents the **LENGTH** of their first loop. If a player rolls a 3, they will need to complete that obstacle three times.

The winner completes the most stations in the **FASTEST TIME**.

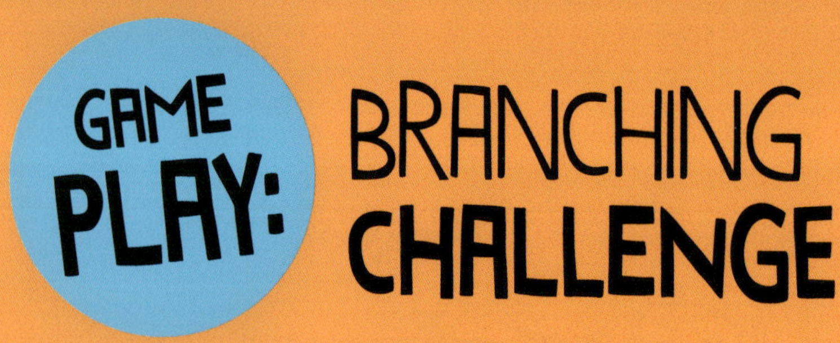

GAME PLAY: BRANCHING CHALLENGE

If you want to add an **EXTRA CHALLENGE**, let's set up a branch for each station.

We are going to make our obstacle course **TRICKIER** by making different **RULES** for completing the course, depending on whether you roll an **ODD** or an **EVEN** number with the die.

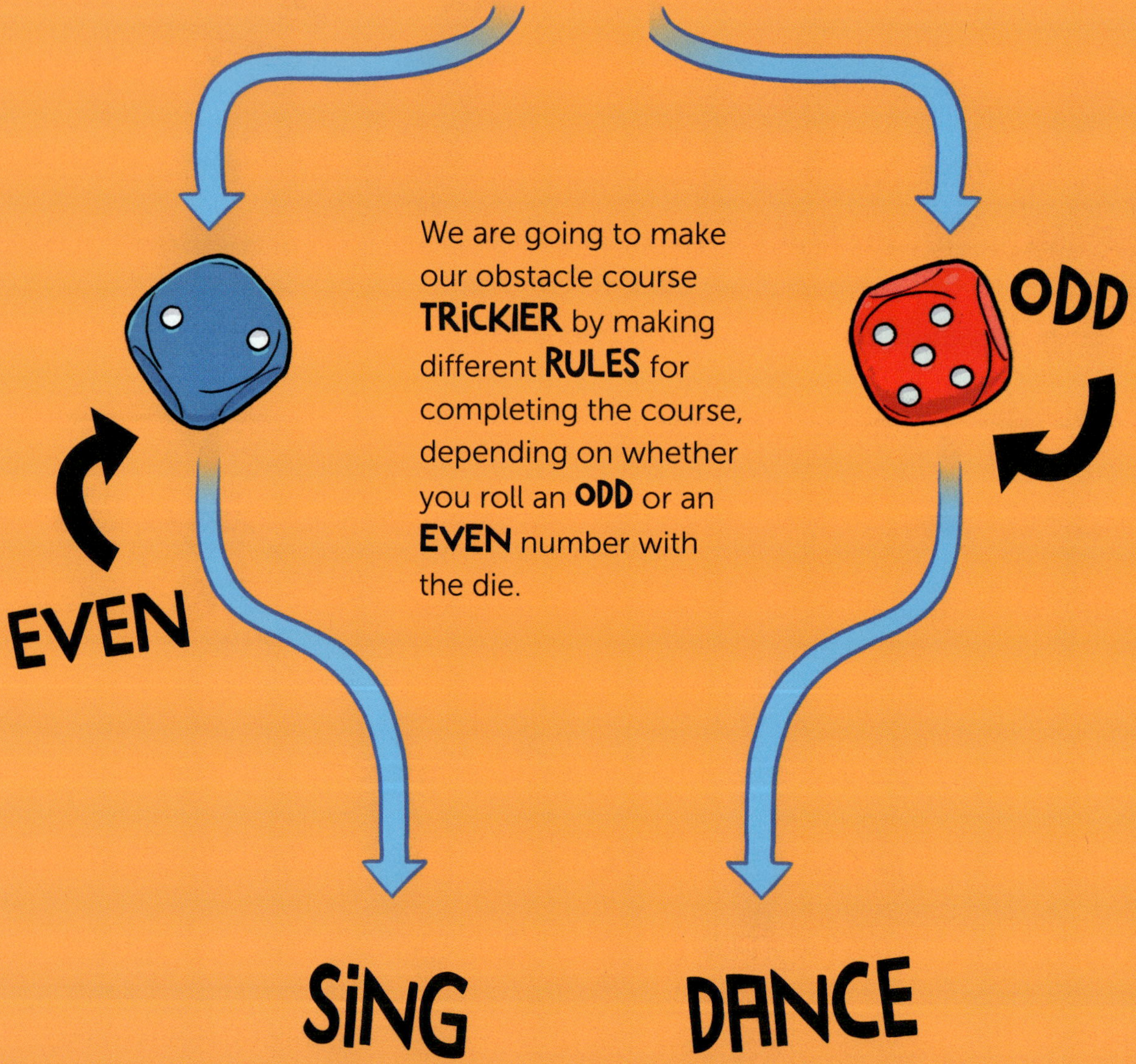
EVEN
ODD
SING
DANCE

For each station, you'll need to think of an instruction for an even number and an odd number. **GET CREATIVE!**

Examples could include:

EVEN:

COMPLETE THE COURSE BACKWARDS.

ODD:

SING THE ABCs WHILE COMPLETING THAT LOOP!

ODD:

COMPLETE IT WITH ONE EYE CLOSED.

EVEN:

DANCE THROUGH THAT OBSTACLE.

Complete the course again using your branches. This time when you roll the die, the number will help you decide on your loop *and* your branch.

FINISH THE ALGORITHM!

There are instructions missing from this carefully coded treasure map. Use those math minds to figure out how to complete this incomplete algorithm.

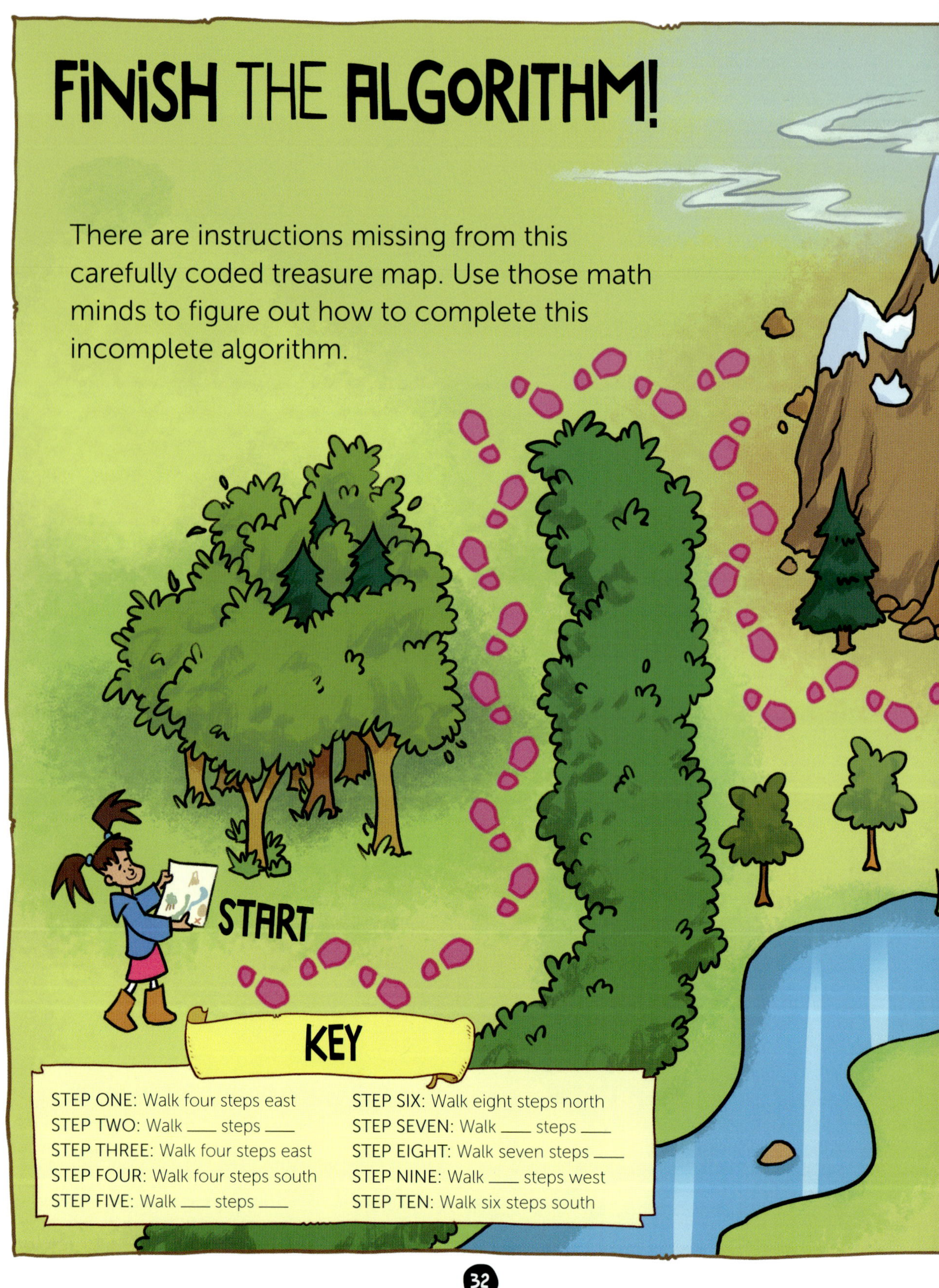

KEY

STEP ONE: Walk four steps east
STEP TWO: Walk ___ steps ___
STEP THREE: Walk four steps east
STEP FOUR: Walk four steps south
STEP FIVE: Walk ___ steps ___
STEP SIX: Walk eight steps north
STEP SEVEN: Walk ___ steps ___
STEP EIGHT: Walk seven steps ___
STEP NINE: Walk ___ steps west
STEP TEN: Walk six steps south

(ANSWER ON PAGE 48)

DECOMPOSITION UNPLUGGED: BUILDING BREAKDOWN

In this activity, we are going to practice our decomposition skills by **BUILDING** and **DECOMPOSING** structures made of building blocks. First, you'll build some awesome structures and then you'll work on decomposing the instructions for your build.

LET'S GET BUILDING!

MATERIALS YOU WILL NEED:

* Building blocks
* Blank paper
* A jar
* A pen
* A group of at least 2 to 4 builders

Let's start by coming up with some ideas for our builds. Work as a **TEAM** to **BRAINSTORM** seven to ten **3D OBJECTS** you could build with your blocks.

WILL IT BE A:

CAR?

TOWER?

BRIDGE?

BOAT?

TREE?

RAINBOW?

PLANE?

HOUSE?

... OR SOMETHING ELSE?

Write down each build idea on a small piece of blank paper.

Fold it up and put it into your jar.

Each player picks a build idea from the jar. Using the bricks, players each build a structure resembling their idea.

Now it's time to **DECOMPOSE THE BUILDS!**

* Give each player a blank piece of paper with the word **INVENTORY** written at the top.

* Players will need to draw or describe each building block they used in their build on their inventory list.

Now it's time to use your counting skills! If the same block is used more than once, this can be represented with a count, for example:

INVENTORY

X 1

X 4

X 2

X 4

X 2

GAME PLAY: ALGORITHM CHALLENGE

Looking for an extra challenge? Create a foolproof algorithm to help someone else build your creation.

Draw out the steps for each brick one at a time.

With your inventory in hand and a clear algorithm, anyone should be able to recreate your masterpiece!

MADE A MISTAKE?

No big deal! We can always "**DEBUG**" our **ALGORITHMS**. If you notice a brick is out of place, simply replace that instruction with the correct one. Players can help one another test their algorithms by swapping lists and giving it a try.

NO BIG DEAL!

SPOT THE BUG!

Spot the mistake in the algorithm below! Which arrow is out of place?

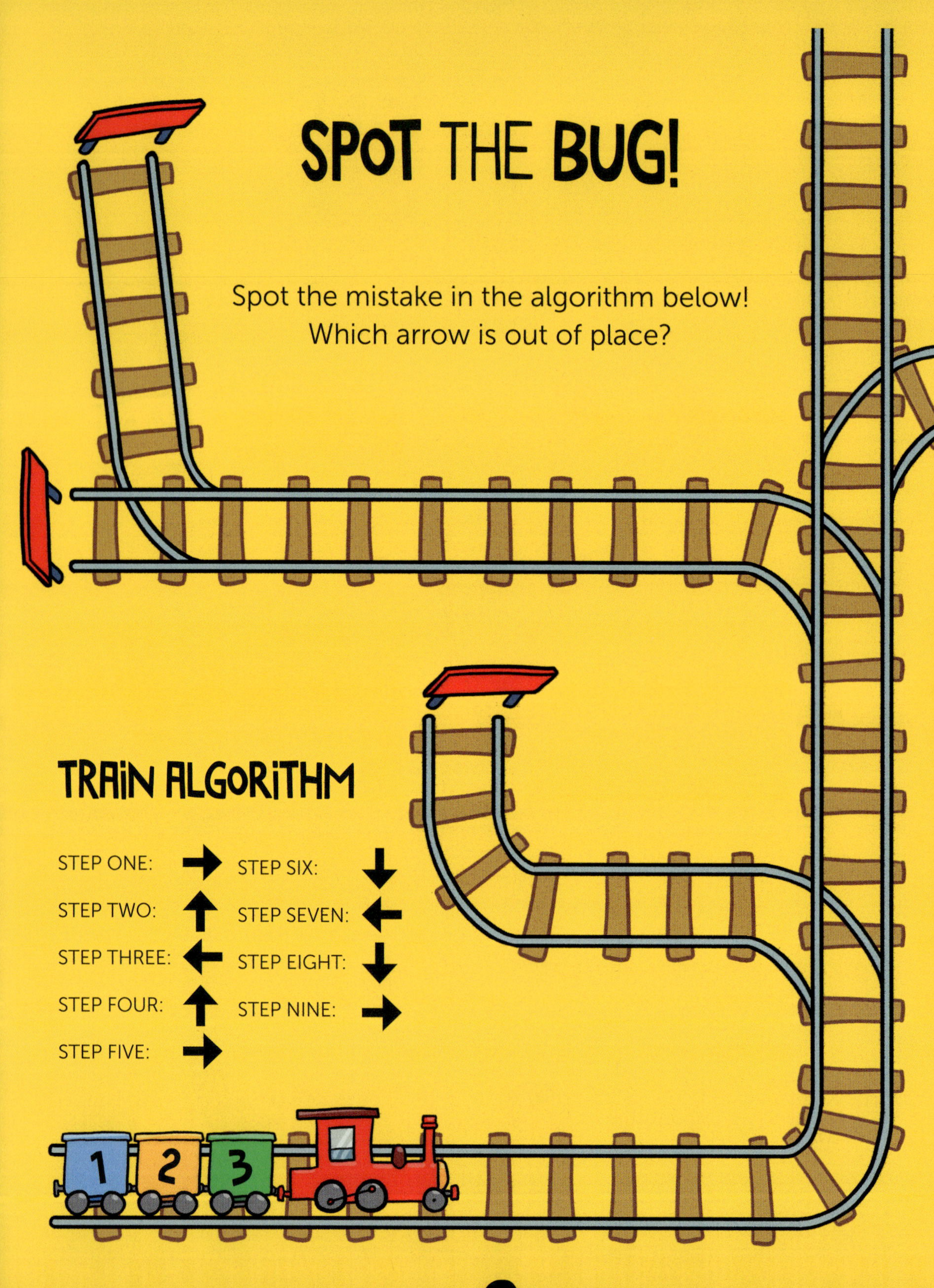

TRAIN ALGORITHM

STEP ONE: →
STEP TWO: ↑
STEP THREE: ←
STEP FOUR: ↑
STEP FIVE: →
STEP SIX: ↓
STEP SEVEN: ←
STEP EIGHT: ↓
STEP NINE: →

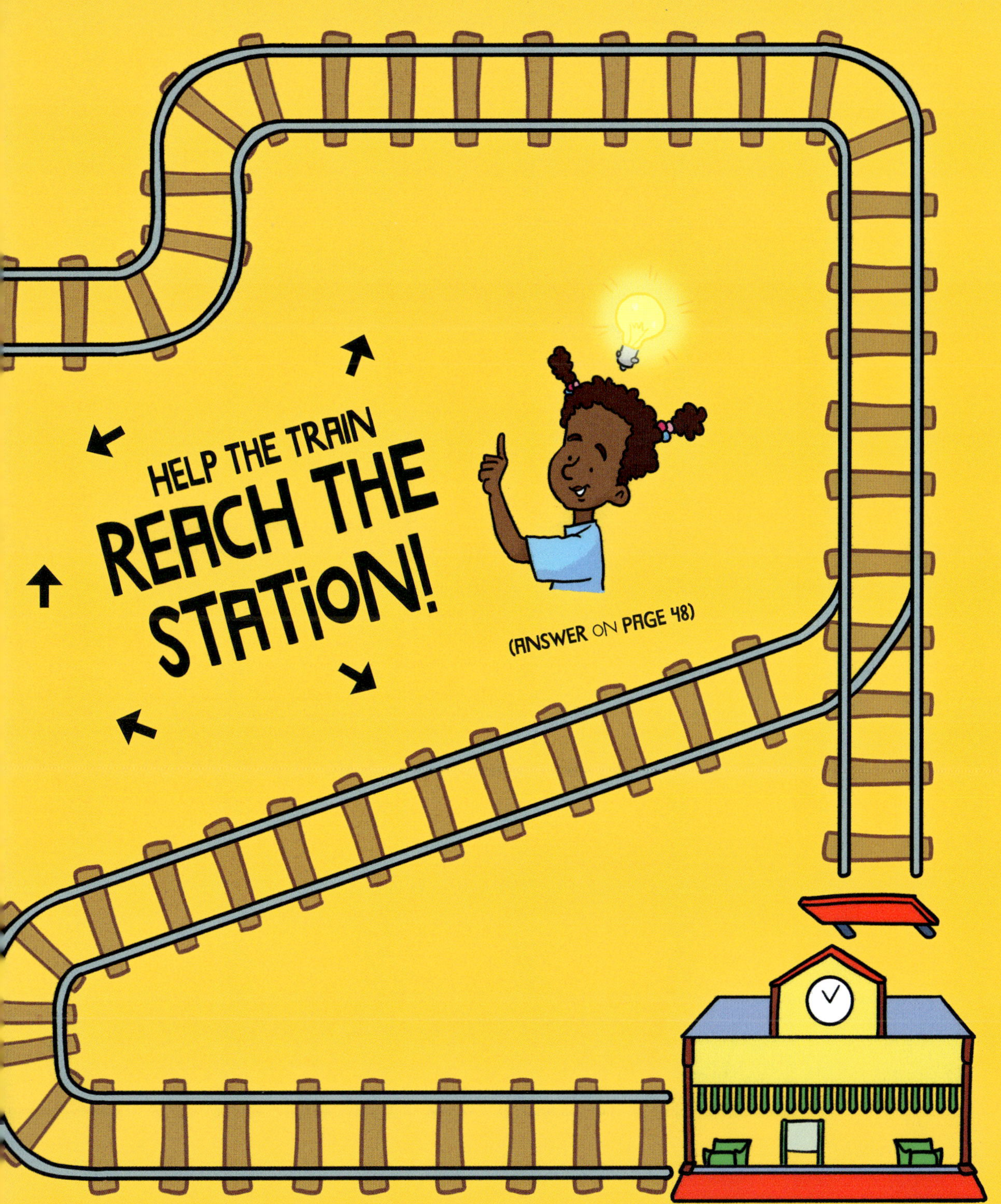
HELP THE TRAIN
REACH THE
STATION!
(ANSWER ON PAGE 48)

LET'S **SOLVE A CODING PUZZLE!**

We've now learned the basic concepts of coding and are ready to think just like a computer.

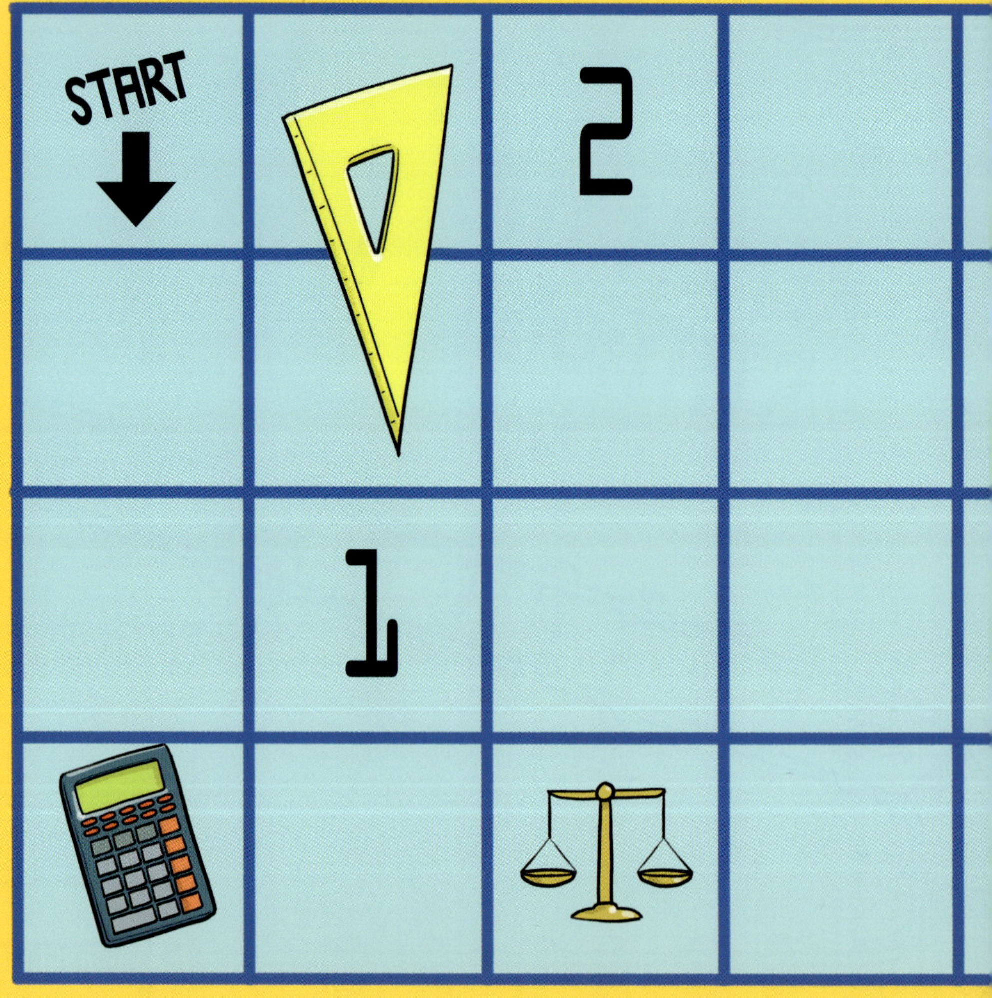

(ANSWER ON PAGE 48)

In this puzzle, we'll need to use our coding and math skills to solve a maze.

Count from one to five in order without running into any obstacles.

Write out the algorithm on a separate piece of paper.

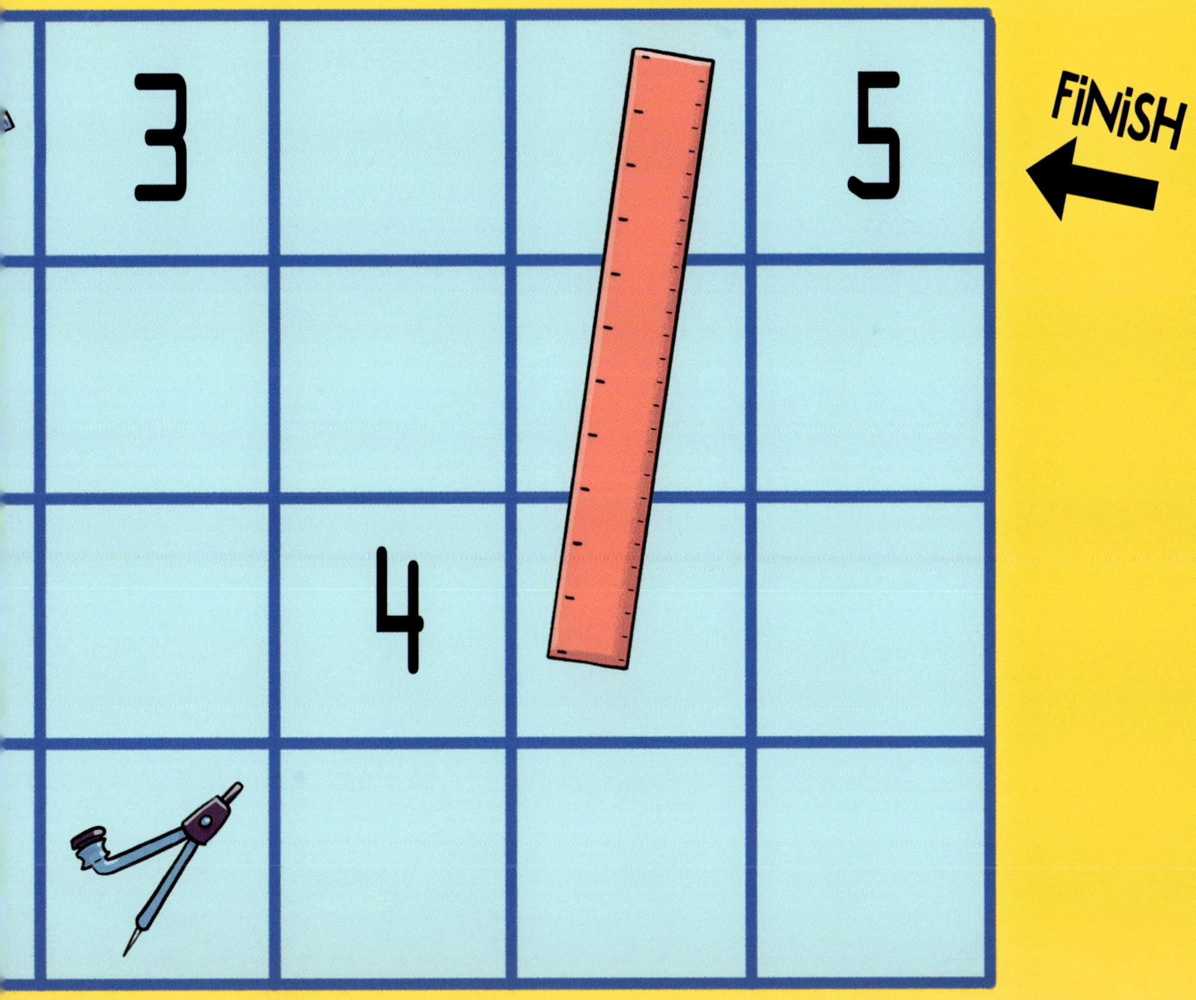

3			5
	4		

FINISH

GLOSSARY

ALGORITHM:

An algorithm is an instruction given to help complete a certain task.

BRANCH:

Branching refers to making a decision based on what is happening or has happened.

DEBUG:

Find and solve a problem in coding instructions.

DECOMPOSITION:

Decomposition means breaking down problems into smaller steps.

INVENTORY:

A complete list of items needed for a job or project.

LOOP:

A set of instructions that repeat until a specific condition is met.

SEQUENCE:

Sequence refers to the order of the steps.

VARIABLE:

A variable is a way of holding information. It's like a box that keeps information inside it.

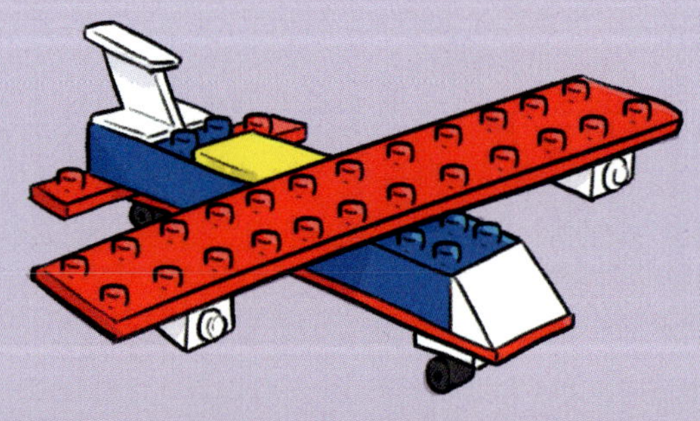

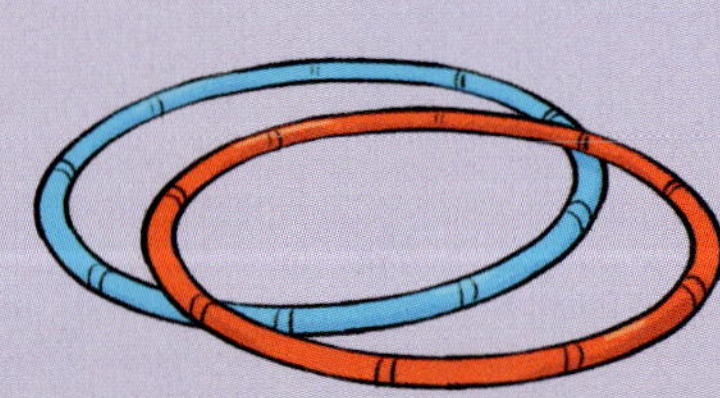

NOTES FOR ADULTS

WHY CODING UNPLUGGED?

Teaching kids to code is a great way to introduce them to the basics of programming and have them learn problem-solving, logic, and critical thinking skills. These skills are applicable in real life, in school, at work, or even while they're playing video games!

One of the best ways to begin coding is to learn to code **UNPLUGGED**, so no computer or other hardware is required! By taking coding offline, it's easy to focus on the basic concepts, which are fundamental to learning to code. Combining coding learning with creative or physical activities is a great way to embed the information and keep children active.

FURTHER INFO

FOR MORE FUN CODING BOOKS, WHY NOT TRY ...

Briggs, Jason R. *Python for Kids: A Playful Introduction to Programming*. San Francisco, CA: No Starch Press, 2023.

Vale, Jenna. *Get Coding with Scratch*. Buffalo, NY: Gareth Stevens Publishing, 2024.

ANSWERS:

PAGE 13:

1+14
2+13
3+12
4+11
5+10
6+9
7+8
(seven ways)

PAGE 22:

The man performing jumping jacks is performing a loop. He repeats the jumping jack movement 20 times until he is done.

The man with the weights and the woman on the mat are performing a sequence. They follow a specific order of movements to complete the exercise.

The dancers are performing an algorithm. They need to remember a specific set of instructions in order to perform the dance movements.

The man holding the plank position is performing a branch. His exercise can be modified based on his skill level.

PAGE 32:

STEP TWO: Walk 7 steps north
STEP FIVE: Walk 9 steps east
STEP SEVEN: Walk 8 steps east
STEP EIGHT: Walk 7 steps south
STEP NINE: Walk 4 steps west

PAGE 42:

Step THREE: should be an arrow facing right

PAGE 44:

Start ➡ 1 Down 2, right 1
1 ➡ 2 Right 1, up 2
2 ➡ 3 Down 2, right 3, up 2
3 ➡ 4 Down 2, right 1
4 ➡ 5 Down 1, right 2, up 3

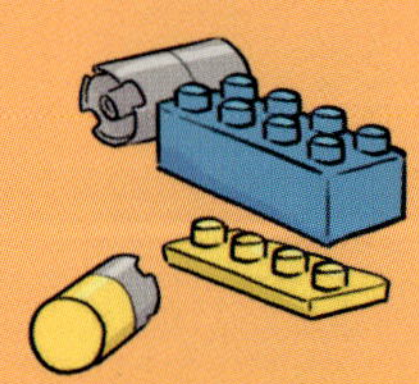